BEYOND
PTSD

BEYOND PTSD

A TRAUMA-INFORMED GUIDE FOR EDUCATORS

BY JESSICA ROOST

CONTENTS

About the author

Introduction

1 Post-Traumatic Stress Disorder (PTSD) and Refugee Children / 2

2 Identifying PTSD / 5

3 The Effects of Trauma on the Ability to Learn / 9

4 Overcoming PTSD Barriers: Sensory Approach / 15

5 Overcoming PTSD Barriers: Cognitive Behavioral Approach / 26

6 Overcoming PTSD Barriers: Mindfulness Approach / 34

7 Other Approaches to Overcoming PTSD Barriers / 38

8 Making a Cohesive Educational Plan for Students with PTSD / 47

Resources

About Tent Schools International

About the author

Jessica Roost is an occupational therapist specializing in pediatric therapy. She received her master's degree from Western Michigan University and has worked in school, outpatient and residential settings. Jessica has completed training in a variety of areas, including relationship-based play, animal-assisted therapy, horticulture therapy, sensory integration and reflex integration. She is a member of the American Occupational Therapy Association and is registered with the National Board for Certification in Occupational Therapy. Jessica has extensive experience working with children exhibiting symptoms of Post-Traumatic Stress Disorder (PTSD) and has traveled to several countries exploring the treatment of PTSD and other mental illnesses. She lives in Grand Rapids, Michigan.

Introduction

Children who have been displaced frequently suffer from Post-Traumatic Stress Disorder (PTSD) after witnessing or being involved in the violence of war or the aftermath of a natural disaster, and being forced to leave their homes. The task of educating children with PTSD includes unique challenges that few educators are equipped to manage. The purpose of this guide is to help educators provide this population of children with learning opportunities that will help them reach their full potential.

By reading this guide, you will gain a better understanding of the following:

1. Possible causes of PTSD
2. How PTSD changes the brain and, consequently, changes the way a child learns
3. How to identify a child who may be struggling with PTSD
4. Various approaches for overcoming the obstacles that impede the learning of a child suffering from PTSD
5. Tips for speaking to parents and the community regarding the special needs of children suffering from PTSD
6. Practical strategies to use within and outside of the classroom to allow for optimal learning for children suffering from PTSD

Chapter 1

Post-Traumatic Stress Disorder and Refugee Children

Post-Traumatic Stress Disorder: the Basics

Post-Traumatic Stress Disorder (PTSD) is an anxiety disorder that can occur in individuals who have experienced or witnessed a traumatic event or a series of traumatic events.

A traumatic event can be any event that is perceived as a threat to one's safety or the stability of one's current environment or way of life. Some examples of traumatic events include, but are not limited to, experiencing or witnessing one or more of the following:

- Physical abuse
- Emotional abuse
- Sexual abuse
- Relocation/separation from family
- Violence
- Death
- War
- Terrorism
- Neglect
- Natural Disaster

After experiencing a traumatic event, it is normal for the human body to react with a stress response. The nervous system is designed to react in this way in order to avoid danger or defend against it. This reaction is referred to as a "fight, flight or freeze" response. Also referred to as Survival Mode, it is an involuntary state of pure stress. While this is a natural response to fear, it becomes a problem if it does not fade over a short amount of time. When the stress response persists, it creates a set of potentially debilitating symptoms that make up Post-Traumatic Stress Disorder.

Post-Traumatic Stress Disorder in Displaced Children

Although PTSD can be experienced by individuals in all populations, its frequency is much greater among displaced people groups. *Displaced children are exposed to more opportunities to endure trauma than is common.* This population of children can experience multiple traumas in all phases of displacement: within their country of origin, while traveling to the site of relocation and during resettlement at a refugee camp or other new location. This vulnerability across a wide range of time, environments and circumstances can lead to cumulative trauma, or complex trauma. Cumulative or complex trauma can be far more difficult to recover from than a singular traumatic event.

Some examples of trauma that displaced children may experience or witness include, but are not limited to:

- Violence
- War
- Lack of basic necessities (food, water)
- Torture
- Robbery
- Injuries and disease
- Physical abuse
- Sexual abuse
- Forced labor
- Betrayal
- Harsh environmental conditions

- Discrimination
- Loss of loved ones
- Loss of property
- Loss of community
- Separation from family
- Persecution
- Harassment
- Poor traveling conditions
- Malnutrition
- Being forced to perpetrate acts of violence or abuse

It is important to keep in mind that in addition to specific traumas such as those listed above, displaced children experience a general loss of control. There is constant uncertainty regarding their futures and there are few, if any, factors in their lives over which they have control. The risk of complex trauma paired with a prolonged loss of control and uncertainty about the future puts displaced children at a much higher risk for developing PTSD than other populations.

As an educator, you are most likely interacting with children during the resettlement phase in which they have already been relocated and are attempting to adjust to their new environment. Often, this is when symptoms of PTSD become more apparent. During the time leading up to displacement, and while traveling to a new location, most children are simply doing what they have to do in order to survive. It is when imminent danger has decreased and they are expected to settle into a new "normal" that one can begin to identify between children who are able to transition out of survival mode and those who may be struggling with prolonged symptoms, indicating possible PTSD.

The following chapter will help you identify the students who are struggling with Post-Traumatic Stress Disorder.

Chapter 2

Identifying PTSD

Symptoms of PTSD vary from person to person, depending on his or her personal experience, support system, environment, level of trauma endured and how his or her unique nervous system is processing that trauma. Symptoms of PTSD also vary depending on a person's age.

It is important to remember that a combination of the following symptoms is merely a red flag for identifying individuals with PTSD. Many of these symptoms could be the results of a variety of other factors and/or developmental phases, which could pass. The list below is not meant to diagnose a person with PTSD; rather, it is a guideline for identifying individuals who may need additional assistance with learning. It is also important to remember that many of these symptoms are normal reactions to stress. It is when they persist beyond three to six months that they may indicate PTSD.

Symptoms of PTSD in Children Ages Three and Under

- **Hypervigilance:** The toddler/child appears abnormally anxious in familiar environments and situations. He/she may appear to be tense or "on edge" in situations in which other children his/her age appear to be comfortable.

- **Frequent crying and/or screaming:** If the child is unable to be consoled during episodes of crying or screaming, he/she may be experiencing flashbacks that he/she is unable to process or verbalize.

- **Separation anxiety:** It is normal for a child up to 12 months to be more attached to certain adults or main caretakers than others; however, if the child appears to be overly clingy past the age of one year, he/she may be exhibiting signs of PTSD.

- **Emotional distress or avoidance in response to nonverbal sensory stimuli:** Children under three years of age form most of their memories through visual images, smells, abrupt noises and tactile information, that is, touch or physical sensation. If the child appears to have an emotional reaction (crying, shutting down, avoidance, throwing tantrums) when in an environment that simulates the sights, sounds, smells and physical sensations of past trauma, he/she may be at risk for PTSD.

- **Difficulty developing to the next stage:** A child struggling with PTSD may be operating in survival mode and may have difficulty transitioning to the next developmental phase, resulting in delayed motor skills, speech, etc.

- **Trouble sleeping/nightmares:** Most babies and toddlers have inconsistent sleep patterns. However, if the child appears to be afraid to go to sleep or wakes up frequently with night sweats, nightmares or night terrors, he/she may be exhibiting signs of PTSD.

Symptoms of PTSD in Children Ages Three to 12

- **Verbalization of flashbacks:** It is normal for children to experience and verbalize intrusive thoughts related to trauma for weeks and months after the traumatic event; however, if a child is experiencing flashbacks three to six months after the traumatic event, it is possible that he/she may be suffering from PTSD.

- **Difficulty trusting others**

- **Re-enacting the trauma through play, repeatedly**

- **Physical illness**: Children struggling with PTSD may have frequent headaches, stomach aches and/or muscle aches. These physical manifestations are not only "cries for help", they are the body's way of processing the release of an abnormal amount of stress hormones.

- **Denial of traumatic event:** If a child actively avoids discussing or processing a traumatic event, he/she may be struggling with PTSD.

- **Difficulty concentrating**

- **Extreme reaction to sensory input:** Children struggling with PTSD may startle easily in reaction to noises naturally occurring in the environment. They may also be hypervigilant to visual stimuli, particularly in their peripheral vision, and olfactory stimuli - smells such as gun powder or smoke.

- **Impulsiveness**

- **Depression or overwhelming sadness**

- **Anxiety**

- **Guilt:** Displaced children suffering from PTSD may feel they could have done more to help others who were harmed.

- **Hopelessness or limited sense of the future:** Many children with PTSD have been living in survival mode for so long that they have limited thoughts or hopes regarding the future.

- **Low self-esteem, self-harm and/or self-destructive choices**

- **Lower cognitive functioning:** Children with PTSD may be stuck in survival mode and unable to access higher-level cognitive functions.

Symptoms of PTSD in Adolescents and Adults

All of the symptoms stated for children three to 12 years of age also apply to adolescents and adults. However, adolescents and adults with PTSD are at a higher risk for:

- **Alcohol and/or drug abuse:** Individuals with PTSD may attempt to self-medicate their emotional pain by relying on drugs and/or alcohol.
- **Suicidal thoughts and/or attempts**
- **Development of eating disorders** or self-harming behaviors
- **Misplaced sexual activity**
- **Isolation**
- **Low motivation**
- **Difficulty maintaining healthy relationships**
- **Poor social skills**
- **Frequently taking risks, or conversely, persistent avoidance of perceived danger**
- **Emotional numbness:** difficulty expressing emotions appropriately, or at all
- **Aggression, agitation, irritability**

Chapter 3

The Effects of Trauma on the Ability to Learn

The human brain is a complex and incredible organ. Our brains seamlessly perform billions of functions on a daily basis. All parts of the brain have to work together to allow us to carry out everything from the most basic of human functions, such as breathing and the regulation of heart rate, to the most complex, higher-level thinking, such as problem-solving, learning, and relating to others. The magnitude of what the brain has to accomplish is immense. When everything works properly, we rarely notice that our brains are doing so many complex and intricate jobs. On the other hand, when something like trauma occurs, there is much that can go wrong. Trauma affects both the structure and the function of the brain, creating a wide variety of challenges in learning, behavior, concentration, emotions and relationships. In order to understand how trauma affects the brain and the way we learn, we must first have a basic understanding of brain development and anatomy.

Typical Brain Development

A baby's nervous system, which will form the brain, starts developing only 16 days after conception. The cells that make up the brain are called neurons. Neurons are responsible for transmitting information via synapses, the junctions between two neurons. At birth, a baby's brain already possesses nearly all of the neurons it will ever have. From birth to age three, the brain is creating synapses at an incredibly rapid rate. The more synapses, the healthier and stronger the brain. By age three, the brain will have billions of extra synapses that are not needed. This is when the brain begins a process called "pruning".

Pruning refers to the strengthening of synapses that are most useful and discarding synapses that are not as useful. For example, once a child begins speaking, the synapses in the area of the brain that control speech begin to strengthen. In order to strengthen the right synapses to form a healthy brain that has the optimal ability to learn, control emotions and control behavior, a child needs the right amount and the right type of sensory stimulation, including touch, sight, sound, smell, taste and movement, within a safe and loving environment. If a child is living in survival mode, among trauma, he or she may be missing crucial opportunities to strengthen important synapses, and those weakened synapses may begin to be pruned. This has serious implications on a child's ability to learn. Before a child with PTSD can learn effectively, he or she will need to transition out of survival mode and strengthen the weakened synapses.

Structures of the Brain

Although the brain is made up of many complex structures, there are a few main structures that concern us as we study the effects of trauma:

Hippocampus: The hippocampus is part of the limbic system, which is the center of the brain that processes and regulates emotions. The hippocampus links memory with emotion. You are most likely to remember situations that involve high levels of emotion because of the hippocampus.

Amygdala: The amygdala is also part of the limbic system. Similar to the hippocampus, it is responsible for emotions and memory. It also plays a large part in survival instincts and emotional behavior.

Prefrontal Cortex: The prefrontal cortex is the part of the brain that is responsible for judgment, decision-making, social behavior and complex cognitive behavior.

Cerebellum: Cerebellum means "little brain". It is responsible for motor control, attention and the regulation of fear and pleasure responses.

Corpus Callosum: The corpus callosum is a structure that links the left and right sides of the brain. It transmits information between the two sides of the brain and is important for regulating emotion, attention and cognitive function.

Cerebral Cortex (Cerebrum): The cerebral cortex is the largest part of the brain. It controls virtually all voluntary movement and higher-level thinking and processing.

The Triune Brain

The theory of the triune brain is a way that neurologists simplify and explain the complexities of the human brain and the effects of trauma.

Reptilian Brain: The reptilian brain is the most primitive part of the brain. It can also be thought of as the survival center. This part of the brain controls the most basic functions of the body, such as breathing, heart rate, blood pressure and digestion. It is also an important part of the "flight, fight or freeze" response. The reptilian brain is fully developed at birth. It includes the brainstem and the cerebellum.

Limbic Region: The limbic region is slightly more developed than the reptilian brain and is typically fully developed between the ages of three and five. The limbic region is responsible for emotions. It contains the hypothalamus and the amygdala.

Cerebral Cortex: The cerebral cortex controls higher-level thinking such as logic, reason, creativity, problem-solving and social interaction. This includes the prefrontal cortex, which controls judgment and decision-making.

Trauma and the Brain

As previously mentioned, trauma changes both the structure and function of the brain. The brain has a natural stress response, which increases certain chemicals such as adrenaline and cortisol. With an influx of these chemicals, a person reverts to survival mode, using the reptilian brain to control reactions. The responses that come from this part of the brain are primitive, involuntary responses that determine whether a person is going to "fight, flight, or freeze". This means that in moments of danger or high stress, a person might react aggressively, flee the situation or shut down completely.

For people who are not exposed to extreme or prolonged stress or trauma, the brain is able to regulate itself. The hippocampus and the amygdala, located in the limbic system, help to level out cortisol and adrenaline shortly after the stress has subsided and the brain returns to a state in which higher-level thinking, taking place in the cerebral cortex, is possible.

People who are exposed to extreme or prolonged stress or trauma have difficulty getting past the reptilian brain, or survival mode. They are stuck in a "flight, fight or freeze" mode and struggle to overcome those immediate stress reactions with emotional regulation (limbic system) or higher-level thinking (cerebral cortex). This means that the brain is so focused on survival that it cannot reach the level of problem-solving, learning, social interaction and emotional regulation. The brain perceives threats that no longer exist, and this inhibits higher-level thinking.

Not only does the brain function differently following prolonged stress or trauma, but the very anatomy, or structure, of the brain changes. Studies have shown that individuals struggling with PTSD have a smaller hippocampus, amygdala, corpus callosum and prefrontal cortex. As you previously learned, these parts of the brain are important for processing emotion, memory, judgment and higher-level thinking.

Summary

The study of the brain and the effects of trauma is complex and difficult to understand, but in learning these concepts, we realize that PTSD is not simply a set of misbehaviors or "mental blocks"; PTSD is truly a disorder affecting the very structure and function of the brain, leaving the person with little control over intrusive thoughts, hypervigilance, anxiety and other barriers to learning.

It is also important to note that studies show that many children with PTSD are particularly hypervigilant to stimuli in their peripheral vision. This is because they are always on the look-out for danger. This chapter outlines strategies to reduce this distraction.

Signs that a child with (or without) PTSD is struggling with Sensory Processing Disorder include:

- Bothered by touch - does not like to be in line, gets overly upset when accidentally touched
- Seeks intense movement and has trouble sitting still
- Sensitivity to lights or sounds
- Overactive/hyperactive
- Appears sluggish or tired
- Seeks certain textures and has difficulty keeping hands to him/herself
- Seeks small, tight, dark spaces
- Experiences behavioral outbursts
- Has "picky" eating habits
- Overwhelmed in busy environments
- Often appears to be distracted

Environmental Considerations for Children with PTSD/Sensory Processing Disorder

There are many simple changes you can make to the physical environment of the classroom in order to help facilitate learning for children with PTSD who are also struggling with Sensory Processing Disorder:

1. **Reduce visual clutter** – Excessive visual clutter (posters, wall art, decorations) can be very distracting for children with PTSD and sensory challenges. Remove unnecessary posters and decorations, leaving only important visual reminders such as the schedule and the rules. If you'd like to display

items such as children's art or motivational quotes, keep them to a minimum and try putting them up at the back of the room so they are not within view for children who are easily distracted. Also, remember to wipe the chalkboard clean when you are finished with the information that was on it. Open bookshelves can also be distracting. If you do not have access to cabinets with doors, try hiding any open bookshelves or storage areas behind curtains or drapes.

2. **Organization** – Effective organization is important for everyone, but especially for those with PTSD/Sensory Processing Disorder. Keep materials organized in predictable places and label them, if needed. Try color-coding for different subjects. If reading/writing is blue, the child's reading/writing folder will be blue, the reading/writing section on the visual schedule will be blue, and vocabulary flashcards will be in a blue box, for example. Give the children a specific folder for assignments that need to be completed in order to avoid losing homework. Leave 10-20 minutes each week to help students re-organize anything that has become messy and to de-clutter desks and tables.

3. **Post a visual schedule** – Posting a visual schedule will help decrease anxiety for those who rely on predictability, it will help keep students organized and on task, and it will ease transitions. It will also be a way to signal to a child which material he/she should have ready. Examples of visual schedules can be found on the website listed in the resource section in the back of this guide.

4. **Boundaries of Physical Space** – Make it clear where group work takes place, where the teacher's space is, and that each student's "home base" (desk area) is for him or her only. If students are having trouble staying within boundaries, tape or chalk can be used to mark out a boundary on the floor as a reminder. An extra square boundary can be taped on the floor

next to the desk for children to remain in during five-minute stretch/movement breaks. Visual examples of taped boundaries can be found on the website listed in the resource section in the back of this guide.

5. **Correct desk and chair fitting** – It is important that each child fits his or her desk and chair correctly so that he or she is positioned in a way in which the eyes, arms and torso are aligned in the most effective way for completing schoolwork. Children with PTSD/Sensory Processing Disorder often have low muscle tone, poor endurance and/or poor attention. If they are positioned incorrectly, work will be more difficult for them to complete. The correct position is to have the hips and knees bent at 90 degrees and the feet flat on the floor. The desktop should be about two to three inches above the elbow if the arm is hanging at the child's side.

If a child is not positioned correctly and you do not have alternate desks and chairs available, get creative in modifying his or her desk and chair. A small stool or box can be placed under the feet so that they touch a solid surface. Books or firm cushions can be placed on the chair if the child needs to be seated higher. A graphic showing correct desk and chair fitting can be found on the website listed in the resource section in the back of this guide.

6. **Create a "safe space"** – Designate a corner of your room as an "escape", "calm-down corner" or "safe space" for children who are overwhelmed or struggling with sensory overstimulation. This space could include a small tent or a curtain to shut out sensory input. It could also be blocked off using a bookshelf, and could include blankets, pillows and other comforting objects. Headphones should also be kept in this space in order to reduce auditory stimuli.

Make it clear to your students that there are rules for the safe space so that it does not become a distraction or avoidance technique. Students must have the teacher's permission to visit the safe space and there should be a time limit set beforehand. Students should go to this space before they are having behavioral problems, in order to prevent escalation. If a student is already out of control, he or she should not be sent to this space.

7. **Create a transition area** – Children with PTSD/Sensory Processing Disorder often have difficulty transitioning. Maintain order by giving plenty of warning before transitions and by designating a transition area for leaving or entering the room. This is an area in which children are expected to line up and to respect the boundaries of their peers. Putting numbers or X marks on the floor with tape can help cue to children where they should stand when lining up.

Instructional Accommodations and Adaptations for Children with PTSD/Sensory Processing Disorder

There are also strategies that can be applied to your teaching methods which may help students with PTSD who are experiencing Sensory Processing Disorder. There are also ways to slightly alter your methods to help facilitate the learning of those with PTSD/Sensory Processing Disorder as well as the rest of the class. These include:

- **Providing multiple means of presentation:** Present material auditorially, visually and kinesthetically.

- **Providing multiple means of expression:** Some of your students with PTSD/ Sensory Processing Disorder may have more difficulty writing out answers or answering verbally, for example. Be creative in how you assess their understanding of the subject matter.

- **Providing multiple means of engagement:** Allow students to engage in ways that are interesting and motivating for them. For example, a child with PTSD may have a specific interest in one area and may be triggered by other subject matter. Use the positive interest to motivate him or her in all subjects by altering story problems in math, for example, to be about that interest.

- **Simplify or supplement existing material** – It is not necessary to have a different curriculum for children with PTSD/Sensory Processing Disorder. By simplifying or supplementing the curriculum you already have, you can accommodate their needs. This could mean altering the format of a worksheet, providing a summary for the child to read before the lesson or providing an outline.

Strategies for Children Having Difficulty Paying Attention and/or Sitting Still Due to PTSD/Sensory Processing Disorder:

1. **Seat the child in an area with the fewest distractions. Create a carrel, or cubicle, on top of his or her desk to block out distractions.** This can be made by taping two folders together or by folding cardboard. Suggested carrel dimensions are a height of 13 inches, a length of 20 inches across the front, and a length of 17 inches on each side.

2. **Provide frequent movement breaks.** This is a great idea for the whole class. Each hour, take five minutes or less to get up, stretch and do simple movement activities. Visual examples of quick movement routines can be found on the websites listed in the resource section in the back of this guide.

3. **Alternate quiet and active**

4. **Reduce the amount of work**

5. **Give extended time for work**, with movement breaks in between

6. **Make the child a "helper"** – have him or her distribute papers, run errands, etc. to keep busy

7. **Break assignments and tasks into smaller parts** and present only one or two parts at a time

8. **Use visuals to keep the child on task** (i.e. break the task down into parts, write the parts down and have the child check them off as they are completed)

9. **Allow the child to hold onto a "fidget"**, such as a small toy or a smooth stone. Explain that it is not to be used as a toy and it will be taken away if used incorrectly. This will help keep the child's hands busy.

10. **Allow the child to sit on a cushion** so that he or she can wiggle without being distracting.

11. **Attach a strip of stretchy material** to the legs of the child's chair so that he or she can quietly kick it to release energy without disturbing others. A visual example of this strategy can be found on the website listed in the resource section in the back of this guide.

12. **Use timers to motivate the child** to stay on task for a certain amount of time

13. **Create a secret signal to cue to the child** that he/she is being distracting. This is a way of correcting the child's behavior without constantly calling his/her name in front of the others and lowering self-esteem.

14. **Similarly, give the child a secret signal** for him/her to let you know that he/she is struggling and needs to step out for a break

15. **Allow changes in position.** Allow the child to stand or lay on his/her belly to do the work, when given permission.

Due to trauma, many children with PTSD have skipped crucial developmental milestones and have difficulty with fine motor skills, visual motor skills and gross motor skills.

Strategies for Students who seem Overwhelmed and/or are having Frequent Emotional Outbursts:

- **Reduce sensory stimuli** - provide headphones to block out excessive noise and create a carrel to block out excessive visual stimuli

- **Allow breaks** to the calming area prior to meltdowns

- **Give the child a weighted lap pad or weighted animal.** These can be made by filling a pillowcase or stuffed animal with popcorn or rice. Weighted objects are very calming to the nervous system and release chemicals in the brain that signal to the child that he or she is safe.

- **Reduce the amount of work**

- **Give the student a certain amount of "break" cards** to trade in for breaks throughout the day

- **Decrease verbal cues and increase visual cues**

- **Be aware of how much time you're allowing for processing.** Some children need extended time to process. If you are instructing a child and he/she is not responding, try not to repeat yourself as this will cause frustration. Give instruction verbally and visually, walk away, and return when he/she has had time to process.

- **Use every opportunity you can to build self-esteem.** Give the student a special job and appropriate praise throughout the day.

Strategies for Children having Difficulty Completing Desk Work:

- **Reduce the amount of writing needed.** For example, modify worksheets to create word fill-ins rather than short answers.

- **Increase the space to write on a worksheet,** or provide extra paper

- **Provide adapted paper** - this could be paper with larger lines, paper with a dotted middle line, or paper with raised lines. You can make raised lines by tracing the lines on paper with glue and letting it dry.

- **Use shorter crayons or pencils** to help facilitate a better pencil grip

- **Provide the child with a slant board** to complete his/her work on. This can be made by clipping the work to a binder.

- **Have the student use graph paper** to line up numbers in math or to help keep letters organized when writing

- **If spacing of letters and words is a problem,** use a popsicle stick or pencil for spacing

- **Reduce visual distractions on the page** by covering up everything except what is being read or worked on. For reading, you can create a window to read through by cutting a rectangle the size of the font out of a piece of paper.

- **Provide the student with an outline** of the lecture or information that will be presented on the board to reduce difficulty and stress from copying information from the board.

Other Helpful Tips and Strategies:

- **Incorporate movement into your day** as much as possible. Create games that turn the subject matter into a movement activity (i.e. children take turns running from one end of the hall to the other to match equations with answers).

- **If a student is having difficulty** interacting with his/her classmates or being part of the group, give him/her a special game or toy to be in charge of at recess that the other students will likely want to participate in (e.g. bubbles, chalk)

- **Avoid taking away recess or gym as a punishment.** All kids need movement! Taking away recess will decrease the ability to pay attention and concentrate.

- **Try to remember that a child does not have to be sitting** in a desk perfectly in order to be learning. For example, a child with PTSD may have to change positions in order to stay calm. As long as he/she is directed to the back of the room and is not disturbing others, the child should be allowed to stay in the room and listen to the lesson.

- **Use buddies!** Pairing students with PTSD with a buddy is a great way to reduce the demand on the teacher and to provide support for the student. As a bonus, the other students who are taking turns being the buddy will learn valuable lessons in patience, compassion and serving others.

- **Make sure every student is successful in at least one thing** every day, no matter how big or small. Commit to ensuring every student leaves knowing that he/she did at least one thing really well that day. This will leave children with a sense of accomplishment and increase their motivation and thirst for learning.

Chapter 5

Overcoming PTSD Barriers Using a Cognitive Behavioral Approach

Cognitive Behavioral Therapy (CBT) is an evidenced-based therapy proven to be very effective in the treatment of PTSD. True Cognitive Behavioral Therapy is conducted by a highly-trained therapist during weeks and months of one-on-one and group therapy. However, by learning about the concepts of CBT and the theory behind it, any educator can easily utilize CBT-based strategies and tools without the extensive training of a clinical therapist.

Cognitive Behavioral Basics

The foundation of CBT is the concept that our thoughts, feelings and behaviors all affect one another. By identifying our thoughts and feelings and replacing negative or irrational ones with positive or realistic ones, we can learn to change our behavior. When we are able to change our behavior, our thoughts and feelings become more positive and realistic. The more a person practices identifying and altering their thoughts and feelings, the more natural it becomes and the more control he or she has over his or her behavior. A graphic demonstrating CBT can be found on the website listed in the resource section in the back of this guide.

Cognitive Distortions

Cognitive distortions, or "thinking errors", are ways that our minds convince us of things that aren't actually true. Although all people experience these from time to time, it is common for people with PTSD to frequently experience cognitive distortions – sometimes to the extent that more of their thoughts are distorted than they are real. These thoughts reinforce negative emotions. Part of using a cognitive behavioral approach is identifying cognitive distortions and refuting them, or proving them wrong.

Some common cognitive distortions include:

- **Filtering:** Magnifying the negative details of a situation and filtering out or ignoring any positive aspects of the situation

- **Polarized Thinking (Black and White Thinking):** If a person is stuck in polarized thinking, everything is an either/or situation. There are no shades of gray and there is no middle ground.

- **Overgeneralization:** Coming to a broad conclusion based on very little evidence

- **Jumping to Conclusions:** Assuming what another person is thinking or feeling and why he/she is acting a certain way without the confirmation of the individual; also, assuming the outcome of a certain situation without evidence that this outcome will occur

- **Catastrophizing**: Expecting disaster, no matter what

- **Personalization:** Believing that what others are doing or saying is in direct reaction to something you've done, and excessively comparing yourself to others

Challenging Cognitive Distortions

Once a person has identified a cognitive distortion, the next step is to challenge that distortion, or to examine it and try to prove it wrong. Some examples of questions that a person can ask in order to examine whether a persistent thought is distorted or not include:

1. Is this thought realistic?
2. What is the evidence for and against this idea?
3. Is there any room for a middle ground (gray area)?
4. Am I focusing only on a negative aspect of this situation?
5. What is the very worst that could happen? What is the likelihood of that happening?
6. What alternatives could there be?
7. Is thinking this way helpful?
8. What are the pros and cons of thinking this way?
9. What would I tell a friend or loved one if he/she told me he/she was thinking this way? Would I tell the person that it is probably real, or give him/her alternative advice?
10. Am I using or thinking in words that are extreme or exaggerated? (i.e. always, never, forever, should, must, need)
11. What are the odds that this is true?
12. In what ways might I be focused on irrelevant or unimportant information?
13. What was the outcome the last time I let myself get stuck on this thought?

One example of a systemic way to track and challenge cognitive distortions to use a chart with four columns. Column headings should be: **Thoughts, Feelings, Cognitive Distortions, and Alternative, Rational Response.** You can use this chart in the following ways:

1. In the table under the **Thoughts** heading, write down a repetitive thought that is interfering with daily life.

2. Under the **Feelings** heading, write the feelings that emerge from this repetitive thought.

3. Use the complete list of cognitive distortions referred to in the resource section in the back of this guide to identify the type of distortion. Enter the name of the distortion under the **Cognitive Distortions** heading.

4. In the last column, under **Alternative, Rational Response**, list reasons why this thought does not reflect reality. The questions on page 28 can help guide the reasoning process.

By tracking and challenging repetitive cognitive distortions, a person can start to "re-train" his or her brain to automatically challenge cognitive distortions. The chart can also be used as a visual reminder of times in the past that a person was able to overcome repetitive thoughts.

By overcoming repetitive thoughts and cognitive distortions, a person can decrease some major barriers to learning, including emotional distraction, anxiety, panic, depression and difficulty concentrating.

Using a Cognitive Behavioral Approach with Children

The concepts presented on the previous pages are clearly too complex for most children to understand. They are presented in this chapter to give you, the educator, a basic understanding for using this approach with your students. The tracking activity using a chart, suggested on page 28, is most appropriate for teenagers and adults. In some cases it could be used by an adult to guide a child through challenging cognitive distortions and track his or her progress. However, there are many cognitive behavioral activities that are better suited for children, outlined on the next few pages.

Practice identifying feelings often. Consider having a morning "meeting" each day before class, when everyone (including the educator) takes turns answering these three questions:

1. How am I feeling today?
2. What is one goal I can make for today? (Encourage children to make goals regarding coping with and/or controlling thoughts and feelings.)
3. Who or what can help me reach this goal?

Here are some other ways to practice identifying emotions:

- **Make a deck of cards with faces and feeling words** on them. You can use these cards to help young children identify their feelings and/or use them to play a couple of games:

    o **Feelings Memory** – Spread the cards out face-down and take turns trying to find matches. When a child finds a match, he/she shares a time that he/she remembers feeling that way

    o **Feelings "Go Fish"** – deal five cards to each player and put the rest in the middle as a "pond". Each person checks his/her cards for matches. When a match is found, the child shares a time he/she remembers feeling that way. Then, taking turns, each player asks another player "Do you have _____ (e.g. worried)?" If the person has the card, he/she gives it to the asking player and then that player shares a memory. If he/she does not have the card, the asker draws from the pond. The play continues until players are out of cards.

- **Use a traditional beach ball with separate sections of color** (i.e. blue, red, yellow) - assign a different feeling state to each color. Play catch with the ball and have the catcher share a time when he/she felt whatever feeling corresponds with the color that his/her right thumb lands upon.

- **In addition to simply identifying feelings, try exploring them in artistic ways.**
    - Have children draw or sculpt how certain emotions (or situations) make them feel. Encourage them to choose colors that they feel correspond with the emotion, and allow it to be as complex, simple or abstract as they want – it does not need to be an actual picture, or image.

- **As "homework", have the students keep a Feelings Journal.** Assure them that the journal will be confidential.

- **Play "detective" using clues such as body language and facial expressions** to guess what one another are feeling. You can also use the detective game to help a student explore his/her own feelings and clues he/she can notice to help give insight into when that feeling might be surfacing.

- **One-to-Five Scale:** In the resource section in the back of this guide is a website with examples of how to utilize the One-to-Five Scale. It is important that children not only identify their feelings, but also understand that they occur on a scale. Some levels of certain emotions are acceptable, while other levels might produce behavior that inhibits learning. Use the charts on the suggested website to explore this scale.

    Also, use the scale frequently in everyday conversation so the children become accustomed to it. For example, as the educator you could say, "This work seems really hard. I think I'm getting frustrated. I think it's at about a 2. Maybe we should all take a break so that it doesn't get to a 5!"

Using this scale will help students have insight into "how much is too much" and when and how to change their behavior based on the intensity of their feelings.

- **When children become increasingly skilled at identifying feelings, introduce the concept of challenging distortions;** however, use kid-friendly language. For example, some pediatric therapists refer to cognitive distortions as *stinkin' thinkin'*. Although it may seem silly, this term helps kids understand that some of their thoughts make them feel "stinky" and that they can work to turn them into positive thoughts.

- **As a class, work together to brainstorm ways to turn intrusive thoughts into more productive or less negative thoughts** (i.e. when thoughts don't go away, find an adult or request a break to take a walk). Post key phrases on students' desks or around the room, such as "I can do it!", "This is hard, but I'll try my best!", "I can change my thoughts!", "Some things are hard, but I am proud of what I can do!", "I don't have to be perfect", "I am safe!", "I am strong!", "I am smart!", etc.

- **Consider having a nonverbal signal** that a child can use when he/she is having a hard time with intrusive or repetitive thoughts. For example, give each child a red card that he/she can put on his/her table or desk when the child is struggling. Then, find a time to discreetly pull that child aside and process those feelings and thoughts with him/her. You can simply listen to what the child has to say, or you can suggest ways to reframe the thought using the strategies mentioned earlier in the chapter.

- **Make up stories to help children understand cognitive distortions.** For example, to help them understand "personalization", you could tell a story about two friends. One friend wanted to play a game with the other friend and the other friend did not want to play. You could ask the children for possible reasons the other friend did not want to play. Point out that there could be many reasons – he/she is tired, he/she has to go home, etc. It is unlikely the reason had anything to do with the friend who asked to play in the first place. You could make the stories even more interesting by using fun animals as characters, role-playing with puppets or kids dressed up as different characters.

Chapter 6

Overcoming PTSD Barriers Using a Mindfulness Approach

Mindfulness and PTSD

Mindfulness is a therapeutic practice used to bring awareness of one's environment, thoughts and feelings in any given moment. Studies have shown that using mindfulness techniques can greatly decrease anxiety and depression, and also significantly increase emotional regulation.

Individuals struggling with PTSD are often mentally and emotionally stuck in the past due to the trauma they have endured. Using mindfulness techniques can keep a person calm within his or her present environment and mental state by focusing solely on what is going on around and within him or herself at no time other than the present. Mindfulness is a helpful approach that aids in switching brain function from "fight, flight or freeze" mode to a more regulated state in which space and attention for learning becomes available.

Using a Mindfulness Approach with Children

Mindfulness can be a difficult concept for children to understand; however, there are many fun, simple ways to engage a student or the entire class in mindfulness activities.

Breathing exercises: When a child is focused on his or her own breath, he/she is better able to regulate emotions and stay "in the moment". The brain is able to move from a "fight, flight or freeze" state to a calm, regulated state. As previously mentioned, once a child is regulated, his or her body and brain are better able to focus on learning.

- Lead the class through some of the breathing exercises suggested on the websites in the resource section in the back of this guide – *balloon breathing, fish breathing and rainbow breathing*. Encourage children to breathe in through their noses and out through their mouths. Try engaging in group breathing exercises at regular intervals throughout the day - when they get to class, before a transition and before leaving school. Each breathing exercise should about five minutes. Increase engagement by allowing students to take turns leading the group in the exercise.

- Along with guided breathing, here are some techniques to help teach children to control their breathing:

    o *Stop and smell the roses* – Have the children breathe in through their noses as if they were smelling a flower. You could encourage their imaginations by having them describe the color and type of flower. You could also have the children make fake flowers to use as props. After they breathe in through their noses, have them breathe out through their mouths, pretending to blow petals or seeds off of the flower (like a dandelion).

    o *Breathe like a bunny* – This is a great technique to use when a child is panicking or having trouble catching his or her breath. Talk about how a bunny's nose moves and twitches fast and have them practice three or four quick breaths in through the nose followed by one long breath out through the mouth.

- *Blow out the candles* – Have the kids take in a big breath, hold it and then take a big breath out, blowing out imaginary candles. Have them hold for a beat before taking the next breath in.

- *Snake breathing* – Breathe in, hold and breathe out slowly using a hissing sound.

- *Using breathing to visualize a change in emotion* - Have the children imagine breathing in something happy, pure and calm (i.e. blue skies with fluffy clouds) and breathing out the bad feelings (i.e. breathing out gray skies).

- *Bubbles* – Blowing bubbles is an excellent way to regulate breath.

- *Peaceful Pals* – give the children stuffed animals and have them lay on their backs with the stuffed animals on their stomachs. Have them breathe deeply, noticing how the animal moves up and down. This encourages deep breathing. Have them picture that they and their pals are breathing in good thoughts and breathing out the negative ones.

Using the senses: Have the children focus on their five senses. Dull the sensory input in their environment enough so that those with sensory sensitivity are not bothered – you can dim the lights, shut off loud fans or have a calming scent available. The children can assume any position they'd like, whether it's lying down or seated. Then they close their eyes and draw their attention to one sense at a time. What do they smell? What do they hear? What do they feel? What do they see in their minds? By paying attention only to what is around them, they may be able to stay in the present and block out traumatic thoughts.

Small fidgets or tools:

- *Worry stone* – Allow children to have small, smooth stones available that they can concentrate on rubbing between their fingers when they need to be brought back to the present and focus on the teacher's instruction.

- *Counting beads* – Have the class make a strings of beads that students can use to "stay in the moment" when their minds are wandering. They can move the beads along the string and count them silently, or add a deep breath for each bead.

Using the body to increase mindfulness: Being aware of your body and the effect of your emotions on how your body feels is an important part of mindfulness.

- *Progressive muscle relaxation* – This is a way to relax the body by tensing and relaxing certain muscle groups at a time.

- *Body scan* – Have the kids lie down, close their eyes and bring attention to each part of their bodies. For example, how does your hair feel? Can you feel your ears? What do your cheeks feel like?

- *Yoga* – Using simple yoga poses is a great way to incorporate movement and calming techniques. Visual examples of yoga poses for children can be found on the website listed in the resource section in the back of this guide.

Chapter 7

Other Approaches to Overcoming PTSD Barriers in the Classroom

We have covered three main approaches to overcoming the barriers a student with PTSD may encounter when trying to learn. However, there a several other factors to consider. All children with PTSD have individual symptoms, strengths, weaknesses and needs. Below are a few additional factors and strategies to consider when instructing a student with PTSD.

Anger Management

When most people think of common side effects or symptoms of PTSD, the first things that generally come to mind are anxiety, depression, and difficulty maintaining concentration or becoming successful in school or other daily activities. However, as an educator, it is important to keep an eye out for children who may be struggling with anger management. These children may be mistakenly labeled as purely having "behavioral issues". Although their anger may be leading to behaviors such as bullying, tantrums, yelling, and showing disrespect to authority, these behaviors are potentially caused by a lack of outlet for anger and a lack of anger management skills.

Displaced children often struggle with anger because it is a psychological response that distracts from other emotions that may be more difficult to process (sadness, grief, worry, etc.). The emotion of anger allows a person to step out of themselves and direct their emotions elsewhere.

Anger, in and of itself, is not a "bad" emotion. It is important that we allow our students to feel anger. They have certainly been through unfair experiences that would illicit an appropriate anger response. It is also important that we help them control anger and direct it in a way that does not disrupt their learning or the learning or their classmates.

An important part of learning anger management is to help a student understand when he or she is starting to become angry. Another important part is to teach children how to gauge the level of their anger, and to find appropriate outlets for it.

Below are some quick ways to control and/or guide a child through the anger he or she is feeling, and avoid negative behavioral responses:

- **Provide a nonverbal cue** that the child can use when he/she needs to take a break (i.e. popsicle stick or card laid on the table)

- **Suggest breathing activities** as described in the previous chapter

- **Tape a sign to the child's desk** (or hang one in the classroom) that reminds them: "It is okay to get angry! It is not okay to: 1. Hurt myself, 2. Hurt others, 3. Destroy property", or something similar

- **Encourage the child to leave the room** and engage in movement activities

- **Encourage the child to draw** his or her anger

- **Allow the child to "destroy" something** that will not be permanently destructive (e.g. playdough, ripping paper) if he/she has escalated to the point of other strategies being ineffective. After the child has calmed him/herself down, process through what happened and possible solutions for next time.

- **Make a "scream box"** that allows the child to let his/her anger out without being too disruptive. Put an empty paper towel tube into a hole in a box after filling the box with Kleenex, towels, or other objects that muffle sound. Allow the child to decorate it in order to personalize it for him/herself. A visual example of a scream box can be found on the website suggested on the resources page in the back of this guide.

PTSD and ADHD

Many children with PTSD either have a known co-morbidity with ADHD (Attention Deficit Hyperactivity Disorder) or, at least, appear to have some of the symptoms of ADHD. We have discussed the way in which a brain with PTSD operates and have learned that the brain is so distracted by being in Survival Mode that it has difficulty accessing the areas of the brain that control concentration, attention and regulation.

Although this often causes symptoms similar to ADHD, it is important to keep in mind that the root cause may be the PTSD. The most effective approach to educating a child with PTSD and ADHD is to use a lot of sensory strategies (see Chapter 4) mixed with CBT strategies (Chapter 5) to address the emotional aspect of the inattentive behavior.

Try to be creative as you incorporate sensory activities with emotional regulation activities. For example, you could turn some of the feelings games mentioned in Chapter 4 into movement games (i.e. assigning different areas of the schoolyard to different feelings and having students hop or run to the one they identify with). *Movement is essential for students with PTSD and ADHD.* The more movement opportunities they receive, the more available they will be to learn.

You may also find that your students with inattentive behavior benefit from frequent changes in position such as lying on their stomachs or hanging their heads upside down over a chair. Another easy change to implement is to assign various tasks to the inattentive student, as if they are your "helper". For instance, you could ask him/her to help pass out papers, retrieve something from another room or collect crayons. Again, it is important to refrain from taking away a student's recess or playtime as a punishment. Children need this time for growth, development and regulation.

Grief Support

Another large part of struggling with PTSD is battling grief. Allow your students to speak openly about their grief and encourage them to talk to other students experiencing similar things.

Flashbacks and Grounding

Many children with PTSD experience flashbacks. A flashback could be experienced as anything from a short memory of a traumatic time to a complete dissociative episode. Dissociation is when a person loses his or her sense of reality because he/she is becoming deeply entrenched in a traumatic memory. This person could appear to be having a panic attack, saying things that don't make sense and/or appearing not to recognize his/her surroundings.

The best way to control flashbacks and dissociation is to have an understanding of the ways in which it may be possible to keep a person grounded. Grounding refers to that person being able to remain within reality. The keys to remaining grounded and avoiding dissociation and flashbacks are to:

- **Try to catch the flashback or dissociative episode before it happens or before it becomes too severe.** The most effective way to do this is to learn a child's triggers and to teach the child what those triggers are and how to avoid them. A child's trigger might be a sudden, loud noise, a certain object or even being backed into the corner of a room. Each person with PTSD has his or her own individual triggers and will likely need help discovering and verbalizing them.

- **Have strategies on hand and easily accessible.** Keep a list of grounding strategies and tools on hand. For example, strong sensory input is a great way to bring someone back to reality. Fill a small container with a strong but pleasant smell and keep the container nearby for use when a student is suffering from flashbacks or dissociation.

- **Have a "safe space" available for students** who may not have caught the episode in time and need some time away. Make sure there is an adult nearby to supervise them.

Proprioception

We often think of the senses as including sight, sound, touch, smell and taste; however, there are two other important senses –vestibular (or movement), which we addressed while discussing ADHD, and proprioception. Proprioception refers to the input to joints and muscles. This includes deep pressure to the skin and muscle, such as a deep hug or a heavy object on the lap. It also includes movement, such as jumping jacks, that puts pressure on the joints as the body contacts the ground after jumping.

Proprioception is an extremely important sense, as it tells our bodies where they are in relationship to the world around them. Proprioception makes us feel *safe*. When we receive proprioceptive input, our brains are flood with serotonin, a natural "feel-good" chemical. This helps us to feel calm, grounded and secure.

Children with PTSD need as much proprioceptive input as they can get in order to feel safe. It can be easy to incorporate proprioceptive input into your classroom routine by taking five minutes here or there to engage the class in some of the following activities:

- Provide deep pressure down through the shoulders
- Encourage the child to crawl into a small, tight space
- Push-ups with variations (e.g. on his or her knees, standing against the wall)
- Plank position with variations (e.g. touching hand to chest and saying a word in a category, letter or number, then switching hands and going to the next word, letter or number)
- Heavy work (e.g. yard work, taking out the trash, raking leaves, moving furniture)
- Bike-riding
- "Push –o-war" (pushing against someone else's hands or legs)

- Playing "statue" (copying different positions that put pressure on joints and muscles)
- Self-hugs (see how tightly they can hug themselves for 15 seconds and repeat as needed)
- Yoga poses
- Roll up tightly in mat or blanket
- Build a fort to crawl in and out of
- Stretches
- Give gentle "squishes", sandwiched in a mat
- Lay on backs and tuck selves in (hugging selves like an egg) for 15 seconds, release and extend arms and legs for 15 seconds, repeat at least five times
- Chair push-ups (lifting selves off of seat or chair using arms)
- Wall pushes with legs or arms
- Use class chairs for heavy work activities (moving them around to use as an obstacle for climbing and crawling, etc.)
- Roll a ball on a student's back as he/she lies on his/her stomach
- Wear tight clothing (or tightly-wrapped blanket)
- Activities using weighted equipment when available. Much of this equipment can be made by stuffing blankets, stuffed animals or a pillow with beans or rice and sewing them up.
- Use of a weighted blanket
- Use of a weighted lap-pad on the lap or shoulders
- Play catch with a weighted ball
- Roll a weighted ball back and forth
- Jumping jacks
- Jumping sideways over a line (make it a game - how fast can they go? Can they criss-cross their legs over the line and then uncross them without touching the line?)
- Running and jumping onto a mat or pile of pillows

- Races that require jumping, hopping or different positions (army crawls, crab walk, etc.)
- Leap-frog (you can use objects to leap over if a student's safety appears to be of concern)
- High-jump competition
- Long-jump competition
- Wheelbarrow races
- Donkey kicks (kicking feet in the air while hands are on ground)
- Tug-o-war
- Take each other for rides by pulling each other around on a mat, blanket, sheet, towel, etc.
- Make an obstacle course with any available items (include crawling, jumping, rolling, etc.)
- Tumbling on a mat
- Crashing on a mat
- Animal walks ("walk like a crab", "walk like a bear", etc.)
- Army crawls
- Run up and down stairs

Therapeutic Art

Art can be a fantastic and effective medium for anyone struggling with emotions, whether the person is dealing with trauma or not. Get creative!

Therapeutic Music

Music can also be a powerful tool for promoting relaxation and attention within the classroom. Explore different types of music with your class and ask them how different tempos and pitches make them feel. Allow them to make their own music with simple instruments. Consider having them make their own instruments and exploring how different noises and rhythms make them feel.

Chapter 8

Making a Cohesive Educational Plan for Students with PTSD

Getting Organized

It is possible that you will have several students requiring some special attention due to PTSD or other mental health issues. It is important to get your students and yourself organized. Visual schedules are a great way to help students keep themselves organized.

There are many techniques to help you, as the educator, keep yourself organized. It is likely that you will use trial and error to find what works best for you; however, here are a few suggestions:

- **Have a binder for each student,** tracking his/her behavior and needs, or have one binder with tabs for each child.

- **Regardless of how you keep your data together, color-coding is a helpful tool.** Assign each child a color and use that color for all of his or her things: the tabs for the notes you keep on the child, the parts of your daily schedule that apply to a certain child (i.e. "Johnny's morning movement break" written in red), a folder used to send notes home, etc.

- **Keep coping materials in one bin** (e.g. anger coping cards, feelings cards, sensory materials) that is easy for students to access as needed. Have a sheet inside which they can use to "sign out" the tool being used.

Taking the extra time to become well-organized will reduce your level of overwhelm in the future.

Keeping Plans Individualized

Remember that each child is an individual with his or her own strengths and weaknesses. Even if two children have experienced similar traumas, as in the case of siblings, they may have very different responses.

Finding the right educational plan for a child with PTSD will take trial and error. It is important to try a wide variety of things from all of the approaches discussed above. It is even more important to keep track of what is working and what is not. Use a data sheet to track successful and unsuccessful interventions.

Keep in mind that it is wise to try an intervention more than once. If it didn't work last month, it's possible that the child has progressed enough for it to be more effective this month.

It has been mentioned several times in previous chapters that certain activities are appropriate to complete as a class. Although this is true, it is important to keep an eye out for a student who may not be ready to participate in what would normally seem like a "simple" activity. For example, if the entire class is participating in a "feelings game" and one student appears to be shy and quiet, allow him or her to simply observe until he or she is ready. Remember to keep the group activities individualized as much as possible by observing students' behaviors and individual needs.

Communicating with Caregivers

Keeping in contact with a student's caregiver is essential to his or her success. Sending home weekly progress reports is ideal. As the child's educator, it is possible that you have become the most knowledgeable person in his or her life about PTSD and its effects on daily life and on learning. Caregivers may look to you for advice regarding how to control behaviors at home. Encourage open and honest dialogue without acting as the child's therapist. Emphasize to the caregiver that as his/her teacher, you can only give advice regarding the strategies that have worked within the classroom. Encourage caregivers to carry over these strategies at home, reminding them that seeking further professional help, if available, is always ideal.

Resources Related to Chapter 3: Identifying PTSD

Websites:

- Functions of brain regions: www.childtrauma.org
- Centers of the brain: www.teach-through-love.com

Resources Related to Chapter 4: Overcoming PTSD Barriers - Sensory Approach

Websites and PDFs:

- Visual schedules: www.theinclusivechurch.wordpress.com, www.brighthubeducation.com

- Taped boundaries: www.educationandbehavior.com

- Correct desk and chair fitting: www.kidzoccupationaltherapy.com

- Quick movement routines: www.rcmp-grc.gc.ca, www.margdteachingposters.weebly.com

- Stretchy material/chair strategy: www.therapyfunzone.com

- Reading window strategy: www.readingwindow.org

- Spivey, B.L. (2013). *Handy Handouts: What is Sensory Processing Disorder?* - www.superduperinc.com/handouts/pdf/399_WhatisSPD.pdf

Book: Moore, K. M. (2005). *The Sensory Connection Program: Handbook.* Farmingham, MA: Therapro, Inc.

Resources Related to Chapter 5: Overcoming PTSD Barriers - Cognitive Behavioral Approach

Websites and PDFs:

- Cognitive Behavioral Approach: www.opencuny.org

- Complete list of cognitive distortions: www.vanderlylegeek.com

- One-to-Five Scale: www.5pointscale.com

- Emotion Word Cards: www.prekinders.com/emotion-word-cards/

- Mini-book: Feelings www.scholastic.com/parents/resources/free-printable/writing printables/minibook-feelings

- Paper Fortune Tellers for Exploring Emotions www.autismteachingstrategies.com/wp-content/uploads/2014/11/CBT-Paper-Fortune-Tellers-for-Anxiety-Other-Issues.pdf

- Monster Emotion Cards: www.professorpoppins.blogspot.com/2013/03/free-monster-emotions-cards.html

- Printable Break Cards www.pbisworld.com/tier-3/breaks/

- The Incredible 5 Point Scale www.pbisworld.com/tier-3/breaks/

- Coping Skills Worksheets
  www.unstressyourself.com/best-coping-skills-worksheets/

- Updated Feelings Book – FREE
  www.chapelhillsnippets.blogspot.com/2012/01/valentines-day-feelings-book-download.html

- Relax Kids Worksheets
  www.relaxkids.com/store/downloads/Worksheets

- Think, Feel, Act Worksheets
  www.teacherspayteachers.com/Product/Think-Feel-Act-Worksheets-2228067

- Unhelpful Thinking Styles
  www.psychology.tools/download-therapy-worksheets.html

- Worry Thought Record
  www.psychology.tools/download-therapy-worksheets.html

- Therapistaid.com – Worksheets and Tools for Mental Health Professionals:
    - "How I Feel"
    - "About Me"
    - "What is Worry?"
    - "Self-Esteem Journal"
    - "_____'s Goal Sheet"
    - "Basic Emotion Assessment"
    - "List of Emotions"
    - "Emotion Wheel"
    - "Where do I Feel?"
    - "My Fears"

Book: Moore, K. M. (2005). *The Sensory Connection Program: Handbook.* Farmingham, MA: Therapro, Inc.

Resources Related to Chapter 6: Overcoming PTSD Barriers - Mindfulness Approach

Websites and PDFs:

- Balloon breathing: www.littletwistersyoga.com

- Fish breathing: www.move-with-me.com

- Rainbow breathing: www.branchhabitat.blogspot.com

- Yoga for children: www.kidsyogastories.com/kids-yoga-poses

- What is Mindfulness? www.psychology.tools/download-therapy-worksheets.html

- Relaxed Breathing: www.psychology.tools/download-therapy-worksheets.html

- Progressive Muscle Relaxation: www.psychology.tools/download-therapy-worksheets.html

- Calm Down Yoga for Kids www.childhood101.com/2015/04/yoga-for-kids/

- Therapistaid.com – Worksheets and Tools for Mental Health Professionals:
    - "Mindfulness Exercises for Children"
    - "Mindfulness Exercises"
    - "Progressive Muscle Relaxation Script"

Book: Moore, K. M. (2005). *The Sensory Connection Program: Handbook.* Farmingham, MA: Therapro, Inc.

Resources Related to Chapter 7: Other Approaches and Factors to overcoming PTSD Barriers in the Classroom

Websites and PDFs:

- Scream Box: www.griefspeaks.com

- TEAR Grief Model
  www.psychology.tools/download-therapy-worksheets.html

- 100 Art Therapy Exercises
  www.intuitivecreativity.typepad.com/expressiveartinspirations/100-art-therapy-exercises.html

- Therapistaid.com – Worksheets and Tools for Mental Health Professionals:
  - "Managing ADHD"
  - "What is Anger?"
  - "Anger Management Skill Cards"
  - "Anger Warning Signs"
  - "Goodbye Letter"
  - "Grief Sentence Completion"
  - "Grief Postcard"
  - "ADHD Checklist for Teachers"
  - "Anger Thermometer"

Resources Related to Chapter 8: How to Plan a Cohesive Educational Plan for Students with PTSD

Websites and PDFs:

- Treatment of Post-Traumatic Stress Disorder: The Cupboard Metaphor
  www.psychology.tools/download-therapy-worksheets.html

- PTSD and Memory:
  www/psychology.tools/download-therapy-worksheets.html

- Intrusive Thoughts: Why do they Persist?
  www.psychology.tools/download-therapy-worksheets.html

- Understanding Child Traumatic Stress: A Guide for Parents
  www.nctsn.org/resources/audiences/parents-caregivers/understanding-child-traumatic-stress

- Trauma Quick-Fact Sheet
  www.studentsfirstproject.org/wp-content/uploads/Trauma-quick-fact-sheet-for-parents-teachers-and-other-child-serving-professionals-2.24.14.pdf

About Tent Schools International™

***Beyond PTSD* is a publication of Tent Schools International,** a non-profit organization providing safe, compassionate learning environments for displaced children. Tent Schools International comes alongside in-country partners in refugee camps and other transitional areas to establish effective schools for children fleeing war, persecution and natural disaster, advocating for displaced families through access to education and other welcoming initiatives regardless of religion, ethnicity or nationality.

Learn more at www.tentschoolsint.org.